# INDIAN CURRENCY

# INDIAN CURRENCY

HENRY DUNNING MACLEOD, M. A.

GYAN

*Published by*

Gyan Publishing House
5, Ansari Road
Daryaganj, New Delhi-110002
Phone: 011-47034999, 9811692060
E-mail: books@gyanbooks.com

*Distribution Network*
gyanbooks.com
India, USA, Canada, UK, Australia, France



ISBN: 978-81-212-8778-4 (PB)
First Published, 1898

2nd Impression 2023

*Printed at:* Gyan Press, Delhi.



**INDIAN CURRENCY**
Author: Henry Dunning Macleod

# INDIAN CURRENCY

# INDIAN CURRENCY

BY

HENRY DUNNING MACLEOD, M.A.

OF TRINITY COLLEGE, CAMBRIDGE, AND THE INNER TEMPLE, BARRISTER-AT-LAW

SELECTED BY THE ROYAL COMMISSIONERS FOR THE DIGEST OF THE LAW TO PREPARE THE DIGEST OF THE LAW OF BILLS OF EXCHANGE, NOTES, ETC.

HONORARY MEMBER OF THE JURIDICAL SOCIETY OF PALERMO, AND OF THE SICILIAN SOCIETY OF POLITICAL ECONOMY

CORRESPONDING MEMBER OF THE SOCIÉTÉ D'ÉCONOMIE POLITIQUE OF PARIS, AND OF THE ROYAL ACADEMY OF JURISPRUDENCE AND LEGISLATION OF MADRID

LONDON

LONGMANS, GREEN AND CO.

LONDON, NEW YORK & BOMBAY

1898

# PREFACE

A Monetary Crisis of the most momentous gravity has arrived in the affairs of India. It has been brought on by a series of measures showing the grossest ignorance of the rudiments of Economics, by successive Governments both Company's and Imperial, which have brought India to the verge of bankruptcy. The Government themselves describe the state of the country as **"intolerable."** Now as the errors of these measures are as glaring and blazing as the Sun of Calcutta at mid-day, it is perfectly possible for the present generation to undo the unwisdom of its predecessors

The present Tract is an endeavor to show how it can be done

The present Monetary System of England is founded on the experience of centuries, and the unanimous arguments of the greatest Economists for 500 years

It is the most perfect Monetary System ever devised by the ingenuity of man. It is now being adopted, with perhaps some slight modifications of detail, by the most powerful and civilised Governments in the world

The obvious thing to be done, therefore, is to bring the Monetary System of India into harmony with that of England and other civilised Governments, and so to improve its commercial relations with the majority of other nations

This Tract is divided into two parts—

The first treats of the means of restoring its ancient and immense Gold Currency to India which it possessed for thousands of years before the fatal 1st of January, 1853, when it was demonetised at a moment's notice by Lord Dalhousie, the most astounding *coup de finance* in the history of the world, and establishing it on solid and permanent foundations for ever

The second treats of the extension of Banking and Paper Currency. But these need not be brought into operation together, because the Gold Currency must first be firmly established before the measures of Banking I suggest can be carried into effect

There are but three courses that can be suggested in the present unfortunate state of the Monetary System of India—

1. To introduce Bimetalism

2. To reopen the Mints to the free coinage of Silver

3. To comply with the unanimous desire of India in 1864 that the Sovereign should be made the Standard Unit throughout the British Dominions in India

After coquetting with Bimetalism for 30 years, in defiance of the weighty and unanswerable Minute of the Governor-General in Council in 1806, the Government have now finally abandoned the vain chimera of introducing Bimetalism into India either by an Act of their own, or by International Agreement

They also absolutely reject the proposal to reopen the Mints to the free coinage of Silver as that would bring instant bankruptcy on the country

There remains, then, only the third and last course—to restore the ancient Gold Currency—which the Government have now declared their resolve to do

A cry has been raised by some persons who are not altogether disinterested, that the Government policy is "tampering with the Currency." But all the Monetary troubles of India have been brought about by unscientific "tamperings with the Currency"

When the East India Company in 1818 changed the ratio of their Coins, and violently forced the Silver Rupee as unlimited Legal Tender on Southern India, whose Currency had been nothing but Gold from the earliest antiquity, they most decidedly "tampered with the Currency"

When in 1835 they gave up the attempt to maintain Bimetalism as hopeless, and made the Silver Rupee the sole unlimited Legal Tender throughout India, and made the Gold Coins receivable at their market value in Silver, they again "tampered with the Currency"

When on the fatal 1st January, 1853, Lord Dalhousie at a moment's notice and with a stroke of his pen demonetised the whole of the immense Gold

Currency, he "tampered with the Currency" with a vengeance

As few of the public are well informed about Indian Currency, I have given in Chapter I. a history of the causes which have led to the present perilous condition of Indian Finance, which will enable them to diagnose the disease

Some persons have been frightened at the supposed vast sum required for restoring a Gold Currency to India, but I have shown that it is very greatly inferior to what may have been anticipated, and that it may be obtained many times over in India itself without resorting to any other market for a single ounce

It is imagined by a not inconsiderable number of persons that Silver only has been the currency of India from time immemorial and that the natives are attached to it. This is, however, entirely erroneous. Silver was first forced upon the entire native population by the Company in 1818, and it was only in 1853 that Silver has been the exclusive currency of India in consequence of Lord Dalhousie demonetising Gold. The natives themselves greatly prefer their ancient standard, Gold

As then the consequences of preceding Governments having forced an exclusive Silver Currency on India have been found to be most injurious to the best interests of the country, it only remains for the present Government to undo the errors of their predecessors, and to restore the ancient Gold Currency and to make the Sovereign the standard unit in accordance with the universal demand of 1864. I venture to hope that I have shown that it can be done with great facility if undertaken with a resolute will and a firm determination. There can be no Monetary peace in India until it is accomplished. It will be one of the most momentous Economical events of the nineteenth century, and it will start India on a new career of prosperity

# INDIAN CURRENCY

## CHAPTER I

## CAUSES OF THE PRESENT MONETARY CRISIS IN INDIA

### Bimetalism

**1.** Mediæval princes conceived that it was part of their inalienable Divine Right to alter the weight and name, and debase the purity of their Coin as much as they pleased, and to compel their subjects to receive the diminished and degraded and debased Coin at the same value as good full-weighted Coin. This was termed *morbus numericus*

Charlemagne established the system of Coinage which was adopted by all the States in Western Europe. For some centuries the Kings of France preserved the original purity and weight of their Coins. But about the beginning of the 11th century they greatly diminished their weight and also debased their purity. This for several hundred years produced the most terrible distress and commotions and political disturbances, and drove away foreign trade from the country. In 1366 Charles V., surnamed the Wise, saw that the only way to restore prosperity to France was to restore the Coinage to its ancient weight and purity. He referred the whole matter to Nicholas Oresme, one of his wisest and most trusted councillors, afterwards Count Bishop of Lisieux, who, in answer to the request of his Sovereign, drew up his now famous treatise "*Traictie de la première invention des Monnoies.*" This is the first great treatise on a question of Economics, and has only been brought to the notice of Economists in comparatively recent years. It now stands at the head of modern Economic literature

**2.** Poland, which then comprehended the modern Prussia, was afflicted with the same evils. Copernicus, who was a member of the Prussian Diet, had long been complaining of the evils brought upon the country by the degradation and debasement of the Coinage. Sigismund I., King of Poland, determined to redress these evils, and applied to Copernicus to aid him. At the instance of Sigismund, Copernicus drew up in 1526 a masterly treatise on Money, which he entitled "*Ratio Monetæ Cudendæ*," which has only been discovered in the present century, and is included in the magnificent edition of his works published at Warsaw in 1854. Copernicus had no knowledge of the work of Oresme, written 160 years before his time, but the principles he laid down were absolutely the same

**3.** The early English Sovereigns did not diminish or debase their Coinage, but they suffered vast quantities of base and degraded Coins to remain in circulation, and consequently all the good and full-weighted Coin disappeared as soon as it was issued from the Mint. Edward I. was the first to diminish the weight of the Coin. He coined 243 pennies out of the pound weight of Silver, and by successive diminutions the pound weight of silver was coined into 744 pennies by Elizabeth. The instant disappearance of the good Coin as soon as it was issued from the Mint was the subject of repeated debates in Parliament for several centuries. It was an inscrutable puzzle to the Financiers and Statesmen of those days. They conceived that the people were inspired by the Evil One to prefer the bad Coin and to reject the good. But they had no Oresme or Copernicus to explain it to them, and the only remedy they could devise was to enact severe penalties of mutilation and death against those who exported good Coin, which penalties were wholly ineffectual

At last Sir Thomas Gresham explained to Queen Elizabeth that good and bad coin cannot circulate together, but that the good coin disappears and the bad coin alone remains current. As Sir Thomas Gresham was the first person in the country to explain that permitting bad coin to circulate was the **cause** of the disappearance of the good coin, I suggested in my *Elements of Political Economy*, published in 1857, that it should be called "**Gresham's Law,**" and this name has now been accepted throughout the whole world. The treatises of Oresme and Copernicus were not made popularly known by my friend M. Wolowski till 1864. Oresme, Copernicus and Gresham independently made it known to their respective Sovereigns, and therefore it ought to be called the Law of Oresme, Copernicus and Gresham

## Gresham's Law.

**4.** The principles laid down by Oresme, Copernicus and Gresham may be summarised as follows :—

(1) That the Sovereign has no right to diminish the weight, or change the denomination, or debase the purity of the coin. To do this is robbery

(2) That the Sovereign can in no case fix the Value or Purchasing Power of the Coins. If he could do so he could fix the value of all other commodities—which was indeed the idea of mediæval princes

(3) That all that the Sovereign can do is to maintain the coins at their full legal weight and purity and denomination

(4) That the legal ratio of the coins must strictly conform to the relative market value of the metals

(5) That if the fixed legal ratio of the coins differs from the natural or market value of

the metals, the coin which is under-rated entirely disappears from circulation, and the coin which is over-rated alone remains current

(6) That if degraded and debased coin is allowed to circulate along with good and full weighted coin, all the good coin disappears from circulation, and the degraded and debased coin alone remains current to the ruin of commerce

(7) That there cannot be two measures of value in the same country, any more than there can be two measures of length, weight or capacity

(8) That if good full weighted coin and base and degraded coin are allowed to circulate together, all the good coin is either (1) hoarded away ; or (2) melted down into bullion : or (3) exported

(9) That when good coins are issued from the Mint, all the base and degraded coin must be withdrawn from circulation, or else all the good coins will disappear, to the ruin of Commerce

**5.** This great fundamental law of the Coinage soon became common knowledge. It is thus stated in a pamphlet of 1696—

" *When two sorts of Coin are current in the same*

*nation of like value by denomination, but not intrinsically* [i.e., in market value] *that which has the least value will be current and the other as much as possible will be hoarded": or melted down into bullion ; or exported, we may add

Or it may be expressed thus—

"*The worst form of Currency in circulation regulates the value of the whole Currency, and drives every other form of Currency out of circulation*"

**6.** This great fundamental law of the Coinage has been found to be universally true in all ages and countries, and was henceforth recognised and acknowledged in all discussions on the Coinage

It applies in the following cases—

(1) If the Coin consists of one metal only and clipped, degraded and debased Coins are allowed to circulate together with good Coins all the good Coins disappear. They are either hoarded or melted down into bullion, or they are exported, and the bad Coin alone remains in circulation

(2) If Coins of two metals such as Gold and Silver are allowed to circulate together in unlimited quantities at a fixed legal ratio which differs from the market ratio of the metals, the Coin which is underrated disappears from circulation, and the

Coin which is over-rated alone remains current

(3) As a necessary corollary it follows that it it impossible to maintain a Fixed Par of Exchange between countries which use different metals as their standard unit

**7.** It is further to be observed that the same law applies to unlimited quantities of Silver, and unlimited quantities of Inconvertible Paper Money, so that we can always argue from one case to the other.

**8.** This law is not confined to single and separate countries. It is not limited in time or space. It is absolutely universal. In the time of Copernicus no one had conceived the idea of two or more countries combining to form a common system of Coinage. But if they did, or if the whole world combined to have a common system of Coinage, they would for the purposes of Coinage be only one country : and it would be equally impossible for a combination of countries, or for the whole world, to maintain Coins of two or more metals in circulation in unlimited quantities at a fixed legal ratio differing from the market or natural value of the metals, as it is for separate or single countries to do so. If, then, the whole world were to agree to rate a Coin below its market value it would inevitably disappear from circulation : for the whole world can no more make nine equal to twelve than any separate State can

For the very same reason it is impossible to maintain a fixed Par of Exchange between countries which use different metals as their standard : because Coins are only received in foreign countries according to the market value of the bullion they contain, and as the value of the metals is constantly changing in the market of the world, so the value of the Coins must equally do so too

### Coins at a Premium

**9.** When the market value of the metal exceeds the legal rating of the Coin, that Coin is said to be at a *premium :* and the premium is the excess of the value in metal above its rated value in Coin. When this takes place the under-rated Coin disappears from circulation in one or more of three ways :—

(1) It is very usually hoarded away. Every tyro in finance knows perfectly well that when a Coin goes to a premium it is at once hoarded away

(2) It is melted down into bullion. Suppose the market value of the bullion is 18 and the legal rating 15. Then as 15 ounces in legal rating are worth 18 ounces in bullion, bullion brokers would collect every good Coin they could and melt them down into bullion. Again, as 18 ounces in bullion is only worth 15 ounces in Coin, no one would bring bullion to be

coined at the Mint while it is at a premium. The Master of the Mint stated in 1816 that during the 56 years of the reign of George III. no more than £64,000 of Silver had been coined at the Mint, because during all that period Silver had been at a premium

(3) It is exported to places where it passes at its market or natural value.

## The Market Value of Gold and Silver falling Below or Rising above the Fixed Legal Ratio

**10.** Princes then at last understanding that they could not control the relative market value of the metals by fixing a Legal Ratio between the Coins, endeavored to conform to the counsel of their advisers and to fix the Legal Ratio between the Coins in conformity with the market value of the metals. This plan was tried for a considerable time, but it entirely failed to keep both metals in circulation simultaneously. A new consequence developed itself. Though the rate between the Coins was fixed as nearly as possible to the market ratio at a certain time, that had no power to prevent the market value from varying. The result was that the market ratio of the metals sometimes rose above and sometimes fell below the fixed Legal Ratio, and the metals alternatively displaced each other from circulation, as the one was over-rated and the other under-rated. The under-rated metal always disappeared and the over-rated metal alone remained current.

Many instances of this occurred: but the most notable one took place in France after the great discoveries of gold in California and Australia

The ratio between Gold and Silver in 1803 was fixed at 15½ to 1. But Gold was constantly at a premium till 1850. Consequently up to that time there was no Gold in general circulation in France. The Legal Ratio was 15½, but the market value was 15¾. When the Gold came in abundantly the market value of Silver to Gold rose to 15⅓: and that apparently slight change from 15¾ below the Legal Ratio to 15⅓ above it, *displaced the whole Silver of France to the amount of £150,000,000, and substituted an equal quantity of Gold for it!*

## True Remedy Discovered by Sir William Petty

**11.** At last, in 1691, in a posthumous work by Sir William Petty, one of the most scientific men of his age, the true remedy was pointed out. He said that **One** metal only should be adopted as the standard unit, and other metals should only be issued as subsidiary to the standard unit. The same doctrine was advocated with great force and at great length by Locke, whose arguments I have given at length in my *Bimetalism:* also by Harris in the middle of the last century : and finally embodied in the great masterpiece on the subject, Lord Liverpool's *Letter to the King on the Coins of the Realm*, published in 1805. As we shall presently see Lord Liverpool's doctrines were at once adopted by the Indian Government in 1806, which had had forty years' experience of the mischiefs of Bimetalism. These doctrines were at length adopted at the great recoinage in 1817, and ever since then this country has enjoyed the most perfect system of Coinage ever devised by the ingenuity of man. And this system of Coinage is now being adopted by the greater number of the Governments of the world

Thus the repudiation of that system of Bimetalism which so many people are clamoring for at the present day was the very foundation stone of Modern Economics. It is among the very rudiments of Economics, and the recrudescence of Bimetalism at the present day is nothing more than the revival of the most ignorant and barbarous Economics of the fourteenth century. It is about equal in wisdom to an attempt to revive the Mosaic Cosmogony

I may refer those who are interested in the question to my *Bimetalism*, in which the subject is treated at much greater length

**Sketch of the History of the Currency of India**

**12.** I have now to apply these considerations to the Coinage of India

I must, however, begin by dispelling two very prevalent errors :—

(1) That India has had nothing but a Silver Coinage from time immemorial: and that it is not possible to change the inveterate habits of a people

(2) That India is too poor to have a Gold Coinage

Both these assertions are utterly erroneous

In the first place it is certain that Gold was the original measure of value throughout all India. India produces large quantities of Gold, but no Silver. Nevertheless from prehistoric times vast quantities of Silver have been introduced into Northern India to purchase Gold. The ratio of Gold to Silver was 1 to 13 in Persia; but it was 1 to 8 in India. The Phœnicians before the time of authentic history brought vast quantities of Silver from Tartessus, and exchanged it for the Gold dust of the Lower Indus, which Sir Alexander Cunningham, the highest authority on the subject, holds to be Ophir

Sir Alexander thinks that silver was first coined in India about 1000 B.C. Many thousands of these early Indian Silver Coins are still in existence. But the Gold was not coined, it was kept as dust and tied up in little bags, which passed current as money. But as Silver was first coined it was considered as the standard, and the Gold dust passed at its market value in Silver. Darius exacted as tribute from the satrapy of the Punjaub 360 talents of Gold Dust which he coined into Dorics. The other nineteen satrapies paid their tribute in Silver

We have no certain information when Gold was first coined in India, but though Gold and Silver were equally current in Northern India there was never any fixed legal ratio between them. Every petty prince issued his own Coinage. The Mahommedans adopted the Silver Coinage as they found it existing. But their conquests never extended to Southern India ; and Gold was the standard in Southern India until 1818, when the East India Company for the first time forced the Silver Rupee upon the people of Southern India as their standard

These historical facts refute the two errors I have mentioned above—that Silver was from time immemorial the standard of India ; and that India is too poor a country to have a Gold standard

Such was the state of affairs when the East India Company extended their dominion over India. It found 994 different kinds of Gold and Silver coins current of different weights and fineness, and whose value was constantly varying from day to day. No one could tell the value of the coins he might hold. In making even moderate payments the parties were obliged to call in a shroff — a professional money changer—to declare the value of each coin. Finding this an intolerable nuisance the East India Company attempted to issue Gold and Silver coins for the first time at a fixed legal ratio, *i.e.*, to establish Bimetalism. But it turned out a dismal failure. In their perplexity they sought the advice of Sir James Stewart, the most eminent Economist of his day, and he drew up for them a most important work entitled "*The Principles of Money applied to the Present State of the Coin of Bengal*," 1772. This work was the most masterly treatise on Coinage which had yet appeared, and in accordance with Oresme, Copernicus, Gresham, Petty, Locke, Newton and Harris, he showed that it was absolutely impossible to maintain Gold and Silver Coins in unlimited quantities in circulation together at a fixed Legal Ratio between the coins different from the market ratio of the metals. He therefore recommended that the Legal Ratio between the Coins should strictly conform to the relative market value of the metals. I conjecture that Sir J. Stewart could not have seen the works of Petty, Locke and Harris, or he would have seen that the plan was impracticable, and so able and clear-sighted a man would have seen that the only true remedy was to have **One** metal only as the standard, and all other coins only subsidiary to the standard. The Company endeavored to conform to the advice of Sir J. Stewart, but with only very partial success

At length in the spring of 1806 the masterly and unanswerable treatise of Lord Liverpool on the Coins of the Realm reached India. The Governor-General in Council immediately took it into consideration, and issued a Minute to the Governments of Bombay and Madras declaring their entire adherence to its principle that **One** metal only should be made the standard as unlimited Legal Tender, but that other metals might be coined and made current at their market value in reference to the standard. They unfortunately selected Silver as the standard. This was the first great error of the Government. They might just as easily have selected Gold, which was current in immense quantities throughout the whole of India, whereas Silver only circulated in Northern India. They detailed the immense losses they had sustained in consequence of the fluctuating values of the Gold and Silver Coins in circulation, and pronounced an emphatic condemnation on Bimetalism, declaring *that it was utterly impossible to maintain a fixed Legal Ratio between the Coins while the market value of the metals was constantly fluctuating*: in strict accordance with the doctrines of the greatest Economists for five hundred years. This Minute is of overwhelming importance, because it is the first pronouncement of the Government of a great Empire on Bimetalism after the bitter experience of its disastrous consequences for forty years. This Minute was buried in the archives of the India Office, but in 1894 the India Office most courteously permitted me to make it public for the first time, and in my *Bimetalism* I have given the parts of it relating to Bimetalism *verbatim.* I also strongly urged that the House of Commons should call for its publication as of decisive weight in the Bimetallic controversy. This has now been done at the instance of Sir Henry Fowler, and it may be had for *2d.*, so that no one is justified in discussing the subject without making himself acquainted with it

The Government of India took no action on its weighty and important Minute of 1806 till 1818, when it issued a new Coinage of Gold and Silver. They changed the ratio of the Coins to bring them to conformity with the market ratio of the metals, and for the first time forced the Silver Rupee as Legal Tender on Southern India where Gold alone had hitherto been the standard for thousands of years. They declared these Gold and Silver Coins to be equally Legal Tender. Thus in spite of the Minute of 1806 they persevered in the vain attempt to maintain Bimetalism

In 1835 the Indian Government gave up the attempt to maintain Bimetalism as absolutely hopeless. They coined Gold and Silver Rupees of equal weight and fineness. These Rupees weighed 180 grains ; 165 grains pure metal and 15 of alloy ; or 11-12th fine, which has been found to form the most durable Coins. The Silver Rupee was declared to be the sole Legal Tender throughout India, but the

Gold Rupees were allowed to pass current, and be received at the Public Treasuries at their market value in Silver

## Lord Dalhousie Demonetises the Gold Currency of India

**13.** The great Gold discoveries which began in 1848 and 1849 seemed likely to cause a great fall in the value of Gold, and Holland in a moment of undue panic hastily demonetised Gold, which it repented of afterwards, and retraced its step

Lord Dalhousie took the same panic, and in the last week of 1852 he suddenly issued a notification that after the 1st January, 1853, no Gold Coin of any sort would be received at the Public Treasuries. By this unfortunate action Gold was totally demonetised throughout India. By this astounding *coup de finance*, utterly without precedent in the history of the world, it was estimated that £120,000,000 of Gold Coin at once disappeared from circulation and was hoarded away. Then for the first time India became solely a Silver using country, and not from time immemorial as many ill-informed persons suppose. This act of Lord Dalhousie has been the origin of all our present monetary troubles in India, and for forty-five years we have been repenting at leisure

## Powerful Movement throughout India in 1864 to have the Sovereign declared the Standard Unit

**14.** The demonetisation of Gold by Lord Dalhousie was soon felt to be a disastrous error, and a strong feeling grew up in favor of the restoration of a Gold Currency. Some minor movements were made, but in 1864 a most powerful and unanimous effort was made through India for the restoration of a Gold currency. By this time the British Sovereign had acquired an immense circulation throughout the whole of India

The Chambers of Commerce of Bengal, Bombay and Madras took the lead, the Bombay Association and others and many high officials and bankers joined in it

The Bengal Chamber of Commerce stated that the introduction of a Gold Currency into India was almost universally admitted to be a positive necessity demanded by various circumstances which had been developed within the last few years ; and the time had arrived when that necessity should at once be recognised by the State, and measures promptly adopted which should gradually, but surely, lead to the adoption of Gold as the general metallic currency of the country, with Silver as the auxiliary

The Bombay Association urged the introduction of a Gold Currency into India, as the existing Silver Currency was no longer adequate for the wants of commerce, which was seriously crippled by its inefficiency. From time immemorial until within the last few years India had an extensive Gold Currency, and the superior convenience of it was fully appreciated by the Natives. The measures taken by the Government had suppressed the Gold Currency, but had by no means extinguished its popularity. The Gold Coins in circulation commanded a considerable premium in the market, and the Natives made an attempt to remedy the deficiency by circulating Gold Bars bearing the stamp of the Bombay Banks. That large quantities of Gold had been discovered in neighboring countries, which would greatly facilitate the introduction of Gold. That the direct trade with Australia was prohibited by the exclusive Silver standard, and the expansion of the commerce of India seriously impeded. That a Silver Currency might have been suitable to the country when its commerce was limited, and payments in the main extremely small, but was very inconvenient when wealth was largely diffused throughout the country and the operations of commerce had become so enormous. The transport of this bulky and cumbersome currency entailed heavy and useless expense on the country, and was a serious impediment to trade. The insufficiency of the existing currency had already caused severe financial embarrassment, and threatened the commerce of India with periodical and fatal vicissitudes. The restoration of a Gold Currency would be most popularly received in India, both from ancient associations and present convenience

The Bombay Chamber of Commerce said that the monetary condition of India was in the most unsound and unsatisfactory condition, and its exclusive Silver Currency was no longer adequate for its vast population. The trade of Bombay had trebled within the last ten years, and last year the aggregate import and export trade alone of Calcutta, Bombay and Madras had amounted to 1,060 millions of Rupees. (How much is it now ?) The resources of India were only then beginning to be developed, and were rapidly extending in all directions. That the special demand of India for Silver did not arise from any predilection for that metal, but was compulsory, and due only to their exclusive and inconvenient Silver Currency. That while Silver was transported from a great distance at heavy cost, Gold might be cheaply obtained from neighboring countries (and now from India itself). Thus the heavy charges on Silver prevented its re-exportation, and thus it lost its reproductive power, and was a serious and unnecessary loss to India. That the exclusive Silver standard and Currency of India rendered direct trade with Australia and other Gold producing districts impossible, and forced a country with abundance of Gold to traverse half the globe in search for Silver before she could pay for our commodities. The superiority of Gold would secure an immediate and intelligent welcome for it in India. The importation of Gold into India had steadily increased for many years, though it was not legal tender. The Natives themselves had devised a rude remedy for the deficiency of the existing Silver Currency by using Gold bars stamped by the Bombay Banks as a Circulating Medium. The exclusion of Gold from the Currency of India could not be justified or be considered other than barbarous, irrational, and unnatural. The only remedy was to introduce a well-regulated Gold Currency into India

The Madras Chamber of Commerce expressed exactly the same opinions as those of Bengal and Bombay, strongly urging the introduction of a Gold Currency, and also a well-regulated Paper Currency

Sir William Mansfield (afterwards Lord Sandhurst) presented a long memorial urging the same views

Several officials, under the instructions of the Government, held meetings in important cities of the merchants, bankers, and city notables. They were unanimous in their approval of the scheme, and had no doubt of its success. They testified that Sovereigns in immense quantities circulated in their districts : that the natives bought them in large quantities. A witness said that the introduction of Sovereigns into Rangoon would be highly beneficial. They were very popular in Burmah, and should be the only coin. A large number of the collectors in

Southern India reported that large quantities of Sovereigns were in circulation in their districts; and that the natives bitterly complained of the losses and inconveniences they suffered from their not being received at the public treasuries

The bankers of Lahore were unhesitatingly in favour of the Sovereign, because it was the Coin most familiar to them, being most abundant, and almost the only one used for equalising the Exchanges; and if a Gold Currency were introduced the cash balances would become much more available, and it would facilitate the adoption of a Paper Currency

But the Lahore bankers were *incredulous as to the possibility of maintaining the relative value of Gold and Silver at an absolutely uniform rate by the fiat of authority*, instancing as a proof to the contrary the fact that although we issue copper at the rate of 64 copper pice for the Rupee, their money-changers invariably realise batta (premium) on giving change for a Rupee, and the amount of this batta varies with the abundance, or otherwise, of copper current Coin available in the market at the time. The same they conceived must take place when change is given for a current Gold Coin

Wise bankers of Lahore! the proposal of the Government was afterwards wrecked on this very point!

Thus at this time the universal demand was that the Sovereign should be adopted as the Standard

Unit throughout India, because there were immense quantities of it in circulation throughout the whole country, and the natives were perfectly familiar with it

Such is a very slight epitome of the immense mass of evidence collected from all parts of India of the unanimous desire of the people to have the Sovereign made the standard unit. Some persons indeed pretend that it is an impossible chimera to restore a Gold Currency to India. But what can persons sitting in their studies in England know about the matter if they will not read the unanimous opinion of the people of India themselves which was published as a Parliamentary paper in February, 1865 ?

### Proposal of the Indian Government

**15.** In consequence of this powerful and extensive movement the Indian Government, on the 14th July, 1864, addressed a despatch to the Home Government requesting them to authorise them to declare that *British and Australian Sovereigns and Half-Sovereigns should be made Legal Tender throughout the British Dominions in India at the fixed rate of 10 Rupees to the Sovereign !*

Such a proposal was foredoomed to failure, because it was pure and unadulterated Bimetalism, a revival of the lowest and most barbarous Economic ignorance of the fourteenth century. It showed that its authors were ignorant of the fundamental principles of Petty, Locke, Harris, Lord Liverpool, the Minute of the Governor-General of India in 1806; and the principles upon which the British Coinage was established in 1816—that **One** metal alone should be adopted as the standard—and coins of other metals should only be subsidiary and Legal Tender to a small limited amount

In answer to this despatch Sir Charles Wood, Secretary of State for India, replied on the 26th September, 1864

He said that their practical proposal was to make the Sovereign and Half-Sovereign Legal Tender in India for 10 rupees and 5 rupees respectively, and *ultimately* to establish a Gold standard and Currency to India as in England and Australia, with a subsidiary Coinage of Silver, the Silver Coins not possessing the intrinsic (market) value they represent, and being Legal Tender only to a certain amount.

It appeared from the evidence that there was a general desire for the introduction of a Gold Currency into India, that the people were well acquainted with the Sovereign, and that its introduction would be well received, that it would circulate freely at 10 rupees, and that it would be a great advantage to have the Sovereign as the common currency of India, England and Australia

But he pointed out that where Coins of two metals, Gold and Silver, are equally Legal Tender, those of the metal which at the relative rating of the two metals is cheapest at any period are thereby constituted the currency, and the metal of which they are made becomes practically the standard at the time ; and further a very slight difference in the relative value of the two metals may change the standard and the whole Currency of a country

This was exemplified in the recent change in the Circulation of France. In that country Gold and Silver were equally Legal Tender. Gold Coins containing one ounce of Gold were Legal Tender for the same sum as Silver Coins containing 15½ ounces

Before the recent discoveries of Gold an ounce of Gold was worth in the markets of Europe nearly 15¾ ounces of Silver. It was, therefore, according to the relative legal rating of Gold and Silver, more advantageous to pay in Silver than in Gold. Silver Coin, therefore, for many years formed the Currency of France, the Gold Coin bearing a premium. Since the recent discoveries of Gold the value of Gold relatively to Silver has fallen to about 15⅛. This difference has rendered it more advantageous to pay in Gold. Gold has displaced Silver, and now forms the Currency and standard in France

[This very slight change in the relative value of Gold and Silver sufficed to drive £150,000,000 of Silver out of France, and to substitute an equal quantity of Gold in place of it. So much for the theories of Bimetalists. Since then another change in the ratio of Gold and Silver has sufficed to drive out the Gold and to replace Silver]

The very same principle applied to India. How was it possible to imagine that the Sovereign could have been a fixed ratio to the Rupee throughout India. Such a measure would be totally inoperative

Sir Charles Wood accordingly quashed this fatuous proposal, which was nothing but the most melancholy ignorance of the rudiments of Economics

## Mr. Hollingbery's Report to the Government of India, 1875

**16.** In 1875 Mr. Hollingbery, assistant Secretary to the Government in the Financial Department, addressed a most able Report to the Government on the consequences which the fall in the value of Silver had then produced on the finances and material progress of India

At that date the price of Silver had fallen to 57½*d.* per ounce. The local value of Silver had not fallen from what it was before the great fall of it abroad. But in the course of time it must fall to its value abroad, though it would take a considerable time to do so. He shows that what was wanted in India was not the withdrawal of Silver as a bullion operation, but the substitution of Gold for Silver in future importation of bullion to settle any balance of trade. The question was, therefore, not what a difference in value between Gold and Silver would suffice to expel Silver, but what would be sufficient to make the importation of Gold into India for Coinage more profitable than the importation of Silver

He estimated the quantity of Silver in circulation in India at 130 millions sterling: and that 60 millions of Gold would be far more than sufficient to restore a Gold Currency

He shows that with a Gold Currency the cost of remitting 15 millions sterling for home charges would never exceed the cost of sending Gold from India to England that is $\frac{7}{8}$ or 1 per cent. But owing to the balance of trade being always in favor of India, the Council Bills would always be at a premium, so that instead of a loss there would always be a profit

He shows that countries which have a Silver Currency which have an adverse balance of trade or borrow in Gold using countries experience a heavy loss in making remittances for the latter countries: for which reason they find it necessary to adopt a Gold Standard, and every new country which adopts a Gold Standard makes the necessity more urgent for the remaining Silver countries to conform to the general custom of the world, and adopt Gold as the sole legal standard. And the effects of this fall will be disastrous to India because it will be the only country in the East which will offer a fixed price for

Silver irrespective of its depreciation abroad, and so it will be flooded with depreciated Silver

By persisting in retaining Silver as the standard of India, the finances and the progress of India would be irremediably injured; on the other hand great financial advantages and commercial good to that country would follow from the adoption of a Gold Currency in India. And it was not a mere fanciful desire of change, but stern necessity which compelled the European States to adopt a Gold Standard. The same principles which apply to European States also apply to India. The postponement of a change to a Gold Standard will not arrest the evils which were in progress from the fall in the value of Silver, while the longer the change to a Gold Standard was delayed the more difficult and expensive, but not the less inevitable, will it be in the end.

This most able report, written in 1875, deserves the most careful study, as every one of its prognostications has been fully verified and intensified. Country after country has adopted a Gold Standard, and even Japan, which was long considered as the fortress of Silver, has been obliged to give up Bimetalism and adopt Gold. When this report was written the price of Silver was 57½*d.*, and the loss on Exchange in remitting for the payment of the Council charges was a million and a half; at the present time the price of silver oscillates about 27*d.*, and the loss on Exchange is eight millions

In 1876 the Bengal Chamber of Commerce, as the rupee continued to fall, addressed a memorial to Lord Lytton to suspend the coinage of Silver. The Government replied that it would be impossible to suspend the coinage of Silver *without at the same time opening the Mints to the free coinage of Gold as unlimited Legal Tender*

## Correspondence of 1886.

**17.** The India Office then took up new ground with the Treasury. The difficulties of Indian finance were constantly increasing, and the Indian Government demanded that a determined effort should be made to settle the Silver question by International agreement. They repeatedly pressed this demand, persistently alleging that the ratio between Gold and Silver might be fixed by International agreement. The Treasury has persistently denied this. Nevertheless, several fatuous International conferences were held to see if anything could be done, but they all ended in smoke, as they were bound to do. Every sound Economist knows that it is just as chimerical to secure a fixed ratio between Gold and Silver by International agreement as for any single State to do so. It would be just as rational to appoint an International conference to square the circle, or to discover perpetual motion. Both of these are known impossibilities. In Economics it is equally a known impossibility to fix by law a ratio between any two quantities which are produced without limitation. It would be just as rational to suppose that because no single State could abolish the law of gravitation, an International agreement might do so

At last in 1893, when the value of Silver continued to fall, and it was expected that the Bland and Sherman Acts would be repealed, which was done, the Indian Government found itself on the verge of bankruptcy, and that India would form the dumping ground for all the depreciated Silver in the world. It then closed the Mints to the free coinage of Silver, and declared its intention to restore a Gold Currency. But just five years have passed away, and it has never hitherto taken any steps to carry its purpose into effect, and of course it has found itself surrounded with constantly increasing difficulties. The whole of this unhappy India business is an everlasting stigma on British Economic and Financial statesmanship of the nineteenth century

I will now show what this lack of Financial statesmanship has cost India. In 1864 the universal demand of India was that the Sovereign should be made the standard for all India. If this had been done India and England would have had a common standard unit, which is the sole means by which a fixed Ratio of Exchange can be established between the two countries, subject of course to the usual fluctuations of commerce. By closing the Mints to the free coinage of Silver, as has been done in England since 1816, and as is now done by the majority of countries, Silver Rupees might have been coined by the Government for internal circulation at the rate of 10 to the Sovereign. But the Governments, Indian and Home, having let that opportunity pass away, the Rupee has been continually falling until it now rests somewhere about 1*s.* 4*d.* It is a fact perfectly recognised by the Indian Government that a fall of a penny in the Rupee necessitates taxation to the amount of £1,000,000 on the people of India to meet her home charges in London. Thus the fall of the Rupee from 2*s.* to 1*s.* 4*d.* costs the people of India £8,000,000 yearly in taxation for the sole purpose of meeting her home charges. Such is the penalty which the people of India have paid for the ignorance of her Governments of the rudiments of Economics

The Government has now put its foot down firmly for the restoration of a Gold Currency, and in the two following chapters I venture to offer the outlines of a scheme by which I think it can be done

## CHAPTER II

# PROPOSED SCHEME FOR RESTORING A GOLD CURRENCY TO INDIA

### Preliminary Considerations

**1.** The Indian Government has finally abandoned all attempts to introduce Bimetalism, either national or international, into India

The principle that "it is impossible for Coins of Gold and Silver to circulate together in unlimited quantities at a fixed Legal Ratio different from the relative market value of the metals," was the first great principle of modern Economics established in the fourteenth century by Oresme. It has been proved to be true by 500 years of experience, and the arguments of a series of illustrious writers. It is now called "**Gresham's Law.**" It is now recognised by the great majority of the powerful and civilised Governments in the world. The contrary doctrine which is "Bimetalism" is now entirely exploded, and the attempt to revive it is like attempting to revive the Mosaic Cosmogony

**2.** It absolutely rejects the proposal to reopen the Indian Mints to the free coinage of Silver. Such a proceeding would probably reduce the value of the Rupee to sixpence, perhaps even lower: and would produce consequences too terrible to contemplate

It is acknowledged that every 1*d*. in the fall of the Rupee necessitates taxation to the amount of £1,000,000 on the people of India to meet its home charges in London. The fall of the Rupee from 2*s*. to 1*s*. 4*d*. has necessitated taxation to the amount of £8,000,000 to meet the home charges. If the Mints were re-opened to the free coinage of Silver the Rupee would probably fall to sixpence, which would necessitate further taxation of £10,000,000, which India would be wholly unable to support, besides the most disastrous consequences in all its internal affairs

**3.** There is no possible way of establishing a stable Ratio of Exchange between England and India, barring the usual fluctuation of trade, except by having a Common Standard Unit between the two countries—which can only be the Sovereign

This is the direct consequence of Gresham's Law

**4.** The State of the Exchanges depends exclusively on the State of the Coin in which they are settled, and the usual fluctuations of Commerce

**5.** If the Coin in which the Exchanges are settled be always maintained at its full legal weight and fineness, they are not in any way affected by the state of any other forms of Currency in a country, however depreciated they may be

**6.** From time immemorial, up to 1st January, 1853, India had an immense Gold Currency in circulation

About 1100 B.C. the Phœnicians imported vast quantities of Silver from Tartessus into Northern India to purchase Gold which was cheaper there than anywhere else

Sir Alexander Cunningham the highest authority on this subject, conjectures that Silver was coined in India about 1000 B.C.

But this Silver Currency never extended to Southern India where the Currency was exclusively Gold until 1818, when the East India Company for the first time forced the Silver Rupee as unlimited Legal Tender upon Southern India

In 1835 the East India Company abandoned the attempt to maintain Bimetalism in India which they had introduced in 1766 with the most disastrous consequences

They then coined Gold Rupees and Silver Rupees of the same weight and fineness. The Silver Rupee was declared unlimited Legal Tender, but Gold Rupees were received at the Public Treasuries at their market price in Silver

In the last week of 1852 Lord Dalhousie issued a notification that after the 1st January, 1853, no Gold Coin of any sort would be received at the Public Treasuries. This notification totally demonetised Gold in India. An immense mass of Gold Coin—estimated by high authorities at £120,000,000—disappeared from circulation and was hoarded away. Thenceforth the Currency of India has been exclusively silver

**7.** In 1864 a powerful and unanimous movement was made throughout India for the restoration of a Gold Currency. At this time the Sovereign had attained a very large circulation throughout India, and the demand from all India was that the Sovereign should be adopted as the Gold Standard Unit throughout the country

In consequence of this the Indian Government memorialised the Home Government to authorise them to declare British and Australian Gold Sovereigns and Half-Sovereigns to be unlimited Legal Tender throughout the British Dominions at the fixed ratio of 10 Rupees to the Sovereign

This was pure Bimetalism, and the Government of 1864 was evidently unaware of the strong Minute of the Governor-General in Council in 1806 utterly condemning Bimetalism after the experience of its disastrous consequences for 40 years

Sir Charles Wood, Secretary of State for India, pointed out to the Indian Government that such a scheme was absolutely impossible, and refused his consent to it

**8.** In 1893, the Indian Government being alarmed at the continuous fall in the value of Silver, and the expected repeal of the Bland and Sherman Acts by the United States, which was done, closed the Indian Mints to the free coinage of Silver and declared their resolve to restore a Gold Currency to

India as the only possible method of putting an end to the Monetary disturbances which have so long afflicted that country

## Possible Impediments to the Scheme

There are only two possible impediments to establishing a Gold Currency in India or any other country

**1.** A large amount of depreciated Inconvertible Paper Money

There is no Inconvertible Paper Money in India

**2.** A permanently unfavorable state of the Exchanges

But the Exchanges have been continuously favorable to India for thousands of years ; except perhaps in recent years since the demonetisation of Gold.

It is therefore impossible to imagine a country more favorably circumstanced for the restoration of a Gold Currency

## Quantity of Gold necessary

The first consideration necessary is the Quantity of Gold required for the purpose

Mr. Hollingbery, a most able and experienced official Assistant Secretary to the Government in the Financial Department, addressed a Report to the Government of India in 1875, in which he said that in his opinion £60,000,000 of Gold would be far more than sufficient to restore a Gold Currency. Whether this estimate is correct or not I cannot say. The Indian Government in its recent proposals seems to agree in this estimate. But I shall presently show that even if it should be largely exceeded the Gold can be acquired with perfect facility

## Draft Tentative Scheme for restoring a Gold Currency to India

I therefore beg to submit the following suggestions as a Draft Scheme for carrying this purpose into effect

**1.** That in accordance with the universal demand in 1864, in as short a time as can be done, the Gold Sovereign be declared to be the Standard Gold Unit throughout the British Dominions in India

**2.** That the Indian Mints be at once authorised to coin Sovereigns and Half-Sovereigns of exactly the same weight and fineness as British Sovereigns and Half-Sovereigns

**3.** That in terms of the Act of 1870 the Indian Mints be declared to be branches of the Royal Mint of London as the Australian Mints are

That the Indian Sovereigns and Half-Sovereigns should have free circulation, and be unlimited Legal

Tender throughout the British Empire, to the same extent that British and Australian Sovereigns and Half-Sovereigns are

That if this proposal be accepted it should be notified at once to the Mints, so that they may make preparations to carry the resolution into effect as soon as possible

**4.** That every person who brings Gold to the Mint should be entitled to have it coined into Sovereigns or Half-Sovereigns as he may prefer, free of any cost or charge, at the Mint Price of £3 17*s.* 10½*d.* per ounce

**5.** That the Government should keep the coinage of Silver entirely in its own hands. The Gold Sovereign being made the Standard for settling the Exchanges, the value of the Silver Rupee can have no effect on them, and the Government can extend or restrict the issue of Silver as it may deem necessary and expedient for the wants of the people

**6.** That after a fixed date, of which due notice should be given, allowing ample time to make preparation, all Mercantile Bills of Exchange and other Debts of all kinds above a certain small amount should be made payable in Gold alone as unlimited Legal Tender

That Legal Tender in Silver should be limited to a certain small amount. In England the limit is £2.

But from the circumstances of India it would probably be expedient to extend this limit—say to £5, or £10—or such figure as the Government on consideration may deem expedient

## Means of Procuring a Supply of Gold

As a means of procuring the necessary supply of Gold I suggest—

**1.** That after a fixed date, giving ample time to importers to make preparation, all Customs' Duties in India should be paid in Gold

This would insure a constant supply of Gold to the Government

**2.** Considerable quantities of Gold are produced from Indian Mines

If the Gold Mining Companies wish to dispose of their Gold raised they must send it to London, thus causing great delay and expense from freight, insurance, and loss of interest

It is a fact that a large part of the Gold at present exported from India consists of the exports of the Gold Mining Companies sent to London

The principal Indian Gold Mines have made great progress within the last few years. Since 1892 they have quadrupled their output. Many new mines have been started within the last year or two, and I am informed that there are known to be extensive gold bearing tracts which have not yet been touched

If the Mints were authorised to coin Gold the Companies would send their Gold to it to be coined, at a great saving of expense and time, and it would get into general circulation in the country

**3.** The ancients got great supplies of Gold from the lower Indus. I am informed that these supplies do not continue at the present day

**4.** It is a notorious fact that for thousands of years the Precious Metals have been continuously pouring into India. The natives have a fanatical passion for Gold and Silver. But instead of converting them into Currency and employing them in promoting industrial operations, they either hoard them away or convert them into personal ornaments

It is an official fact that from 1835 to 1885 £131,000,000 in Gold were imported into India, and this import has continued ever since

It is known that the exports of Gold from India have been comparatively insignificant to the imports. I conjecture that a large part of the Gold exported from India consists of new Gold raised from the mines and sent to London to be coined.

No person could be so fatuous as to pretend to give any exact computation of the amount of Gold hoarded away or worn as personal ornaments by the natives. But it is something enormous. Persons of the highest authority estimate it at £300,000,000 and upwards

Some persons allege that one of the hardships inflicted upon the natives by closing the Mints to the free coinage of Silver is that they are not now able to convert their hoarded Silver and personal ornaments into Rupees in case of necessity

But the natives prefer to have the greater part of their hoardings and personal ornaments in Gold rather than in Silver ; and the hoarding of Gold has been greatly promoted by the increasing premium on it as compared with Silver

If the Mints were opened to the free coinage of Gold, the alleged hardship caused by closing them to Silver would be entirely obviated

I think that the Government might greatly encourage the natives to bring their hoarded Gold and personal ornaments to the Mint to be coined by offering them a slight advantage for doing so

I cannot doubt that if the natives could have their hoarded Gold and personal ornaments coined into Sovereigns and Half-Sovereigns they would greatly prefer them to their equivalent in Rupees, and thus a great Gold Currency would be restored to India as of old

**5.** It is known that since the great fluctuations in the Exchanges the flow of British capital into India has been greatly arrested if not entirely stopped, because Capitalists may lose all the profits of their investments by a sudden change in the Rate of Exchange

If the Exchanges were rectified by adopting a Gold Currency the flow of Capital from this country would be resumed, industrial enterprises would be undertaken promoting the wealth and prosperity of the country. The remittances from England would counteract any unfavorable Exchange to India

The indirect losses to India from the stoppage of the flow of Capital to India for so long a period must have been immense, probably not less than the direct losses from the fluctuations of the Exchange

Without going too minutely into the calculation I conjecture that the direct losses to India by Exchange since 1861 when the rupee was at 2*s*. cannot have been less than £100,000,000

As Mr. Hollingbery showed, if a Gold Currency were restored to India the Exchanges would be uniformly favorable to her, and instead of making heavy losses on her home remittances she would make constant profits

**6.** For thousands of years until 1st January, 1853, India possessed an immense Gold Currency. At the latter date it consisted of a vast variety of Native Gold Coins and the Company's Gold Rupees. It was then suddenly demonetised by Lord Dalhousie, and it has been estimated that £120,000,000 immediately disappeared from circulation

Every Economist knows that under such circumstances the demonetised Coin is hoarded away. There must be vast quantities of this Gold Currency still in existence and hoarded away by the Natives

Up till 1st January, 1853, all this Gold Currency was received at the Public Treasuries, and in payment of Taxes at its market value in Silver Rupees

I suggest that all this Gold Currency should at once be restored to circulation at its exact equivalent value in Sovereigns

I suggest that the Indian Government should publish a Tariff stating the exact value of each of these Gold Coins in relation to the Sovereign: and that they should all be received at the Public Treasuries, and in payment of Taxes and Private Debts at their Government valuation

I suggest that all such sums received at the Public Treasuries, and in payment of Taxes, should at once be sent to the Mints to be coined into Sovereigns and Half-Sovereigns

By this means these Gold coins will gradually disappear from circulation and be replaced by Sovereigns and Half-Sovereigns, and it would be a great convenience to the Indian community to have a uniform Coinage instead of a vast multiplicity of native coins of different weights and fineness

From these several sources an abundant supply of Gold could be obtained to restore a Gold Currency to India without going to any Foreign Market for a single ounce

**7.** It is well known that the difference between the Standards has greatly impeded the growing commerce between India and Australia. If the Gold Currency were restored to India it would give an immense impetus to its commerce with Australia, and would doubtless bring a large amount of Australian Sovereigns into circulation in India and increase its Gold Currency

## Advantages of these Proposals.

In my opinion the proposals I suggest would have these advantages :—

**1.** They would leave the present Rupee Currency absolutely untouched

**2.** They would supply a mass of Gold many times exceeding the quantity necessary to restore the Gold Currency from the Gold already existing in India itself, without the necessity of seeking an ounce from any foreign market

**3.** They would greatly facilitate the commerce between India and all other departments of the Empire

**4.** They will retrieve the lamentable error of Lord Dalhousie in demonetising the Gold Currency of India—and the lamentable error of the Indian Government in 1864 of meeting the universal demand of India, by proposing to declare Sovereigns universally exchangeable at the fixed ratio of a Sovereign for 10 rupees—which have been the cause of these Monetary troubles which have so long afflicted the country

**5.** They would establish a solid and permanent Monetary System in India for ever.

**6.** They would greatly tend to consolidate the Empire

## On Fixing the Ratio between the Sovereign and the Rupee

The importance then comes as to fixing the Ratio between the Sovereign and the Rupee

So far as Economics is concerned, the amount of Silver being strictly limited, the Government may fix the Ratio between the Sovereign and the Rupee at any figure they please They might fix it at 10 Rupees to the Sovereign if they pleased. But whether it is desirable to do so is another question

It has been alleged that the restoration of a Gold Currency would be injurious to the interests of the Ryots. But I am informed by a high Indian official that throughout the greater part of India the rents are collected from the landlords or proprietors: and that it is only in a small part of India that the rents are collected directly from the Ryots. Besides I cannot see how my proposals can be injurious to the Ryots, because I suggest that the existing Silver Currency should be left entirely untouched: and only to add a Gold Currency to it

The fixing of the Ratio between the Sovereign and the Rupee is so profoundly complex a question that I do not offer any suggestion respecting it. It must be left to the decision of the Government after full consideration of all the circumstances of the case.

There seems to be a consensus of opinion among experts that the most advantageous ratio would be to make the Rupee equal to 1*s.* 4*d.* and 15 Rupees to the Sovereign

My friend Mr. Stewart Keith Douglas, formerly a prominent member of the Calcutta Chamber of Commerce and the Indian Currency Association, and a very keen supporter of the restoration of a Gold Currency and making the Sovereign the standard Unit, shows the advantage of this rating. If it were adopted we should then have—

| | | |
|---|---|---|
| One anna | = | one penny |
| ½ anna | = | one halfpenny |
| ¼ anna | = | one farthing |
| 240 annas | = | £1 |

which would tend to assimilate the English and Indian Monetary Systems

## Change of Monetary System by Government.

When Governments make changes in the Monetary System of a country which they presume to be for the general benefit of the State, they never consider their effects on the interests of private persons. It would be impossible for them to do so

I suggest that the Indian Government should enter into negotiations with the Native Princes and endeavor to persuade them to adopt the Sovereign as their Standard Unit. I am persuaded that they would soon be brought to perceive its advantages. It would unify the Monetary System of India, and greatly facilitate commerce between the Native States and the British dominions

I am of course aware that strenuous opposition will be made to these proposals, but I have not thought it necessary to examine any of the loose statements in the papers. When objections are formulated by responsible parties in definite terms I shall hope to be able to show that all objections to them are untenable

## Chapter III

# ON THE EXTENSION OF BANKING AND PAPER CURRENCY IN INDIA

Intimately connected with the establishment of a solid and permanent Gold Currency in India is the extension of Banking and Paper Currency

It is too much the habit of persons who write on the subject to maintain that Gold and Silver are the only means of ultimately discharging and liquidating Debts

This, however, is an entire error. We have long passed through the ages of Gold and Silver in this country. We are now in the age of Paper—or Credit

All Mercantile and Trading operations in this country with the most infinitesimal exceptions, are now carried on by means of Rights of action, Credits or Debts, and the whole mass of Credits in every form both written and unwritten, constitutes a portion of the Circulating Medium or Currency infinitely exceeding Gold and Silver, and acts upon Production and Prices exactly in the same way as an equal quantity of Gold and Silver

"Credit," says the great American Jurist and Statesman, Daniel Webster, "has done more, a thousand times, to enrich nations than all the mines of all the world"

The great System of Credit is, however, too vast a subject to be exhibited at full length here. I have set forth the whole of the great Juridical Theory of Credit and its practical operations in Mercantile Credit, the colossal system of Banking in its various forms, and the Theory of the Foreign Exchanges, in my *Theory of Credit*, and I must refer readers who wish to study it in its full extent to that work. I will merely say that the future progress and prosperity of India greatly depends on the cautious and gradual development of a solid system of Banking

But there is one small part of it which I must just touch upon here

In the English Mint Gold is coined free of all charge or cost. But as considerable delay may take place before this can be done this involves a loss of interest

The Bank Charter Act of 1844 provides that any person may bring Gold to the Bank, and shall be entitled to demand Bank-Notes in exchange for it at the rate of £3 17*s*. 9*d*. per ounce

I suggest that the Indian Government might enter into arrangements with the Government Banks at Calcutta, Bombay, and Madras to adopt an analogous plan

I suggest that the Indian Government might

have Notes prepared from its own designs, with the names of the respective Presidencies stamped on them from £1 and upwards

That the Government should supply these Notes to the Presidency Banks at the same cost as they pay for their own private Notes

That the Presidency Banks should issue these Notes solely and exclusively in exchange for Gold at the rate of £3 17*s.* 9*d.* per ounce

That the several Banks should be bound to pay these Notes in Gold on demand as the Bank of England is

That these Notes should be made unlimited Legal Tender in their several Presidencies of Issue

That they should be the first charge on the assets of the Bank

These Notes would I think quickly obtain the confidence of the community and diminish the demand for actual Gold

Thus the people of India would enjoy the same advantage that the people of England do. They would be able to convert their Gold at once into active Currency at the cost of 1½*d.* per ounce

The Government would be under no responsibility for the payment of these notes

I have thus endeavoured to adapt the really valuable parts of the Bank Charter Act to the proposed Indian Paper Currency and to avoid its fatal error

It is an entirely exploded fallacy to suppose that Credit can be controlled by imposing fixed limits on the issues of Banks

It is a maxim well known to Bankers that in a great Commercial Crisis—"An excessive Restriction of Credit causes and produces a Run for Gold"

We have had a long series of Commercial Crises since 1793, and in each of them it was proved that an excessive restriction of Notes brought on a Monetary Panic

The Bank Charter Act is founded on the fatal error that Credit can be controlled by imposing a fixed limit on the issue of Notes by the Bank

In 1847, 1857, and 1866 it is notorious that the Commercial Crises were deepened into Monetary Panics by the legal limitation of the Bank's power of issuing Notes

As soon as the Bank was given unlimited powers of issuing Notes *at a very high rate of Discount* the panics vanished in a few minutes

In 1856 I was in the Directorate of a Bank, and saw all the operations of Banking going on before my own eyes

I then investigated the whole history of Monetary Panics, and from circumstances that came to my knowledge, which had never appeared to my knowledge in any book, I brought to mathematical demonstration that the true supreme method of controlling Credit and the Paper Currency was by adjusting the **Rate of Discount** to the state of the Bullion in the Bank and to the state of the Foreign Exchanges

This principle is now universally acknowledged to be the true one. One day at the Political Economy Club Sir John Lubbock observed to me that it was the greatest discovery of the age

I trust that in organising a Paper Currency for India it may be founded on this principle and not upon the fatal error of the Bank Charter Act of imposing a fixed limit on the issue of Notes by the Bank

Many persons connected with various Indian industries contend that it is an advantage to have a constantly "depreciating Currency." This however in the long run is quite fallacious. Such ideas would lead to increasing issues of Inconvertible Paper Money, which always bring on ruin. Some individuals may reap temporary profits from a depreciating Currency because they pay their laborers in the depreciating Currency and sell their products for Gold. But a depreciating Currency is always attended by a general rise of prices. The consequence of the fall in the value of the Rupee has been a corresponding rise in the prices of all European commodities, which has been a most severe tax on our officials. In a general rise of prices the wages of labor are always the last to rise, and during this period the heads of these industries may make large profits. But in process of time this rise reaches the wages of labour, and then these profits vanish. Then a fresh depreciation of the Currency is called for, and so on

What is wanted for the advantage of the country is not a depreciating Currency, but an ample supply of Currency equal in value to the standard at low rates. This can only be done by the extension of Banking. There are still ill-informed persons who suppose that Banking advances are made in solid Cash. But bankers never make their advances in Cash. All banking advances are made in **Credit**—but in Credit convertible into Cash if required, and therefore of the Value of Cash. And it is the stupendous powers of the great Banks in this country, together with the admirable organisation of the System of Credit, which have brought down the Rate of Discount for a considerable period to 1 per cent., and even lower than that. All commercial and trading operations in this country are now effected by Banking Credits and not by Cash

It is by the cautious and gradual extension of Banking and the development of Banking habits among the people that the future progress of India in wealth and prosperity is to be promoted. The current works on Economics are utterly defective in the exposition of the Juridical principles and the organisation of the System of Credit and their application in practice in Mercantile Credit, the colossal business of Banking and the Foreign Exchanges

It would, of course, be quite impossible to exhibit the juridical Theory of Credit and its practical application in this Tract. But I have given the complete exposition of the subject in my "Theory of Credit." This I may observe is not the work of a private irresponsible writer. Having been trained in Mercantile Law by Mr. Edward Bullen, one of the most able and accomplished lawyers of his day, I was selected, after a competitive examination among the members of the Bar by the Law Digest Commissioners, to prepare the Digest of the Law of Credit. The Law Digest Commissioners entirely approved of the Principles of Credit I set forth, and they were afterwards affirmed by the unanimous judgment of the Court of Exchequer in the case of *Goodwin v. Robarts*, and recommended to be put in a form adapted for popular circulation, and shortly after that by Statute became the Law of the land.

Side by side with the juridical Theory of Credit I have exhibited its practical application in Mercantile Credit, the mechanism of the various kinds of Banking and the Foreign Exchanges, and shown how the prosperity and wealth of Scotland have been acclerated by her admirable system of Banking. Of course it is only in the very distant future that such a system can be extensively developed in India.

But it is as well to set before the administration of the country the principles and effects of the system so that they may promote its gradual and cautious progress in India.